TO THE FEW ISRAELITE SISTERS

To The FEW Israelite Sisters

Rehearsing the Righteous Acts, While Awaiting Yahawashi's Return

AHCHWATH MARASHANA

Achwath MaraShana

Copyright © 2022 by Ahchwath MaraShana

All rights reserved. No part of this book may be reproduced in any manner whatsoever without written permission except in the case of brief quotations embodied in critical articles and reviews.

First Printing, 2022

All praises to The Most High Yahawah Bahasham Yahawashi. Double honors to the apostles, elders and teachers of Great Millstone who are out there risking their lives, now more so than ever, to teach this word. To the hopeful elect of the Nation of Israel scattered around the globe that may look and sound like the other nations, to the brothers that are out here pushing this word, and to the FEW sisters trying to attain this knowledge in truth... and of course, to my husband, my covering, my lord, the true love of my life. King Brandon. To you, I say Shalawam!

LETTER TO MY SISTERS

A LETTER TO MY SISTERS (Ahchwath) IN THE TRUTH

To my ahchwath, my dear kinswomen:

I was 28 years old when Yahawah bahasham Yahawashi opened my eyes to the truth. I honestly still believe that I am unworthy of the knowledge The Most High blessed me with, but at the same time, I am extremely grateful. This book I am writing is for every Israelite female. African Americans, Hispanics, Native Indians and others that may be scattered throughout the Earth. The true bloodline of Jacob/Israel. Esau's kingdom wasn't meant to last forever. Once this wicked kingdom ends, our righteous one will begin. The road I was on was definitely heading for destruction. Learning the truth about our heritage has made me such a better woman. I have lost a lot, but gained so much more. My faith was tested back in 2017, but just as Job kept his faith, I never lost mine. This road is not easy. It is the toughest, most strenuous and grievous road you will walk on. You MUST have faith in our power Yahawah bahasham Yahawashi and endure unto the end, He will save you from the coming destruction. I am not wealthy, I am not living my dream life. I am just a humble servant from Detroit trying to do my best to kiss the son, lest he be angry, as is stated in Psalms 2:12. I do pray that you, my ahchwath, stay rooted in Yahawashi, and be willing to accept the knowledge the Most High wants you to receive. So grab a pen, highlighter, or whatever you need to take notes as we search the scriptures to uncover hidden knowledge that has been kept from us for far too long.

Your Ahchwath in Yahawashi,
MaraShana

WARNING

WARNING!! This book is not meant for everyone. Majority of women will absolutely hate some of the truth that is mentioned, but there are **a few** that will actually look at these scriptures through spiritual eyes... **All evidence is backed up with scripture and not made up stories.** Do not be discouraged if you are new to the fold. Our father and savior loves us very much and wants us to receive this knowledge. Brace yourselves as we uncover customs and scriptures that the traditional church will never show or break down to its female members.

This book uses the TRUE HOLY names of YAHAWAH, who the world ignorantly calls God, and HAMACHIAC YAHAWASHI who the world ignorantly calls Christ or Jesus.

Sirach 18:9
They that were of understanding in sayings became also wise themselves, and poured forth exquisite parables.

CONTENTS

DEDICATION
v
LETTER TO MY SISTERS
vii
WARNING
ix
INTRODUCTION
xiii

~ I ~

Learning the Truth
1

~ II ~

The Israelite Marriage
10

~ III ~

Customs of the World
19

~ IV ~

From Women Come Wickedness
25

~ V ~

Conducting yourself as an Israelite Woman

31

~ VI ~

Longing to be a Wife

42

~ VII ~

Israelite Woman Summarized

49

~ VIII ~

Yahawashi's Coming Quickly

58

~ IX ~

Romans 13:11

62

~ X ~

12 Tribes Chart

65

INTRODUCTION

MaraShana

Names meant alot when the world first began. Physical as well as spiritual characteristics contributed to each name our forefather Israel named his sons and the future tribes they would father. (See 12 Tribes chart back of book) Now sisters, I am not here to teach about the different tribes of Israel, but when you dive into biblical as well as secular history, you will see that each tribe matches what our forefather named them. Back in May of 1986, my spirit made its way back to hell for final judgment. (Now if you do not understand that we are in the last days or final judgment, it is my prayer as you read through this book, you will take notes and gain knowledge of the times we are in.) Once I learned the meaning of my name in Hebrew, I felt I must have made many mistakes in my previous lives to deserve the Hebrew name and life The Most High chose for me. MaraShana means Bitter Lily in Hebrew. Mara meaning bitter and Shana meaning lily, or Yahawah is gracious. (Actual word Shana means year but the Hebrew name means Lily/ Yahawah is gracious). Growing up I never understood why my father chose that name for me. People always teased me, telling me that Marshana was a "ghetto name", so for a long time, I hid my middle name.

Bitter comes up a few times in the Bible and it often refers to women, a stale, sour taste, pain, pleading or revenge. When you google the word bitter the second definition comes up as: (of people or their feelings or behavior) angry, hurt, or resentful because of one's bad experiences or a sense of unjust treatment. I am immediately drawn to that definition. Angry, hurt, or resentment because of one's past experiences. Before I learned and accepted that Yahawah bahasham Yahawashi is my one true savior, Mara (Bitter, the first part of my name) completely ruled over my life. I would always go to church, pay tithes, and cry at altar calls just to be depressed Monday through Saturday. My fellow church goers always told me, "If you just believe in Jesus, doors will open for you!" However, it seemed like every time I saw an open door and began praising Jesus, not only did it slam shut in my face, it knocked me so far off that front porch, I always re-emerged with new bruises imprinted in my mind filled with anger, hurt, and resentment. **Ruth 1:20 And she said unto them, Call me not Naomi, call me Mara: for the Almighty hath dealth very bitterly with me.**

No soon after I withdrew myself from the traditional church, I felt my spirit connecting to Shana (Lily, or Yahawah is gracious, the second part of my name). I then started to feel a sense of purity in my spirit. I started learning the Word of Yahawah the way it was written. My spirit always rejoiced when I came down and saw my hubby watching one of the elders' lessons. I felt after I repented for all of my unrighteous acts throughout the years, The Most High actually had mercy on me. Like, He has given me another chance to get things right before the return of Yahawashi. I really feel in my spirit I was called by our Heavenly Father, but I continuously beg and plead everyday that I am one of the few who are chosen. **Matthew 22:14 For many are called, but few are chosen.** I will always accept my full name. The Most High could not teach me how to be righteous until I confessed all my wrongdoings. *Song of Songs 2:2 As the lily among thorns, so is my love among the daughters.* Now that my spirit has fully awakened, I can share the knowledge I have received with the hopeful elect women of Yasharahla on how to conduct ourselves biblically as a TRUE woman of Yahawah bahasham Yahawashi.

For the past seven years, I have devoted my life, not only to the true Lord and Savior, but also to a man The Most High gave a promise too. My husband prayed to have a help meet in these last and final days. It is very important for me to explain the relationship I have with my husband, and how we got together, to understand why I treat him like the King that he is. I met the love of my life at our childhood church when I was about 12 years old. He was a senior in high school, so of course he never noticed me. Fast forward, I'm now in the army, in my early 20s, and my mom invited me to church. I will never forget that day. I knew he was working in the parking lot but I decided not to speak to him. For almost 10 years this man has not spoken to me or anything. I would ask for hugs and he would always say no, or just completely ignore me. This day was different, I guess he saw how much I had grown. He finally makes his move and we have our first official date. At this time, he was new to the truth and excited to tell all the secrets of the Bible. However, I was just infatuated that he finally wanted to talk to me. Yes, I thought he was a little off the wall, but I didn't care. I just knew this was the same man that didn't give me the time of day before and now we were going out. Unfortunately, the military kept us separated up until 2014.

After praying for a wife, my husband heard a message, "If you build it, she will come." He purchased a house and believed that The Most High would send him a wife. He began renovating everything that was needed for the house with only the help of a close friend and his father. During this time, my military service was extended by six months and I was miserable. I cried everyday praying that I could just go home. When I finally medically retired from the army, I was so elated but knew I did not want to stay with my parents. I ended up at a friend's party celebrating her son's graduation and my husbands father walked up to me. I don't remember his father saying hello to any of his relatives, he just walks directly up to me and asks, ``Does my son know your home for good?" Long story short, his father gave him my number and we have been together ever since. We have been biblically married for 7 years and I could not be happier.

The first time my husband sat me down to show me the true scriptures of the Bible, everything just made sense. He went into the curses of so-called black people - **Deuteronomy 28:15-68** the color of the Most High - **Daniel 10:6, Revelation 1:15, Rev 2:18**, reincarnation - **Ecclesiastes 1:9-11, 2Esdras 14:35, Sirach 41:3** as well as the chariots - **Ezekiel 1:4.** Not to mention A LOT of other gems that had my mind completely blown. I will admit, for the first six months I kept asking him to teach me more about women and what the bible says about us, but he continually told me I wasn't ready. At that time I had no idea he was trying to spare my feelings and keep me from running from this truth. It wasn't until I started really doing research years later on women and how they are viewed that I understood why. By the time I finally broke down how The Most High and the nation of Israel viewed the Israelite women in today's society, especially those of the tribe of Judah (so called black women), I was already at the stage where I knew in my spirit that it didn't apply to me. There were plenty of times I learned something and would cry for days because I felt that The Most High would never forgive me, but that just gives me another reason to stay focused on my walk and always plead for forgiveness. **Romans 3:23 For all have sinned, and come short of the glory of Yahawah;** In this society, we have all sinned tremendously in the sight of the heavenly father. Before realizing that we are indeed Israelites, we have all fallen into the hands of this wicked world, and afterwards, you see that it is impossible to keep the laws of our father in the land of our captivity.

Now, I want to make this perfectly clear, this is not a relationship advice book. I do not like to offer advice to women because I have no idea what may be going on in your household. However, our place in this world is to be a wife and I will give you 100% scriptural evidence of how our ancient ancestors dealt with the issues we are struggling with today. My emotions are not writing this book, my knowledge of the truth is. It is a woman's job to teach the younger women how to be wives, and how to be keepers at home. A lot of our issues today stem back to women wanting to be the head of the house and not accepting the order that The Most High arranged. If it wasn't for my husband, I would still be walking in the ways of the world, thinking my ancestors are of African origin.

There are alot of good Israelite men out there waiting for their pillar of rest. The Most High blessed me with a true man of Yahawah bahasham Yahawashi, who has been receiving the word and 100% true doctrine for well over 15 years now and to this day, I have no idea why he chose me. I am not sure why The Most High decided to have mercy on me, but I am forever grateful. It is my hope and prayer that I help my Israelite sisters understand the scriptures that will be brought out and (if you have a husband) to be that pillar of rest our covering needs during these last days. As long as you do not lose your faith in The Most High and accept as well as apply the scriptures to your daily lives. *2 Chronicles 7:14 If my people, which are called by my name, shall humble themselves, and pray, and seek my face, and turn from their wicked ways; then will I hear from heaven, and will forgive their sin, and will heal their land.* We are Yahsharahla, called by Yahawah bahasham Yahawashi, we must humble ourselves, pray, seek his face and turn from the wicked ways of the world; only then will the Most High Yahawah will hear from Heaven, forgive our sins and heal our land. Just knowing that we are called simply by our royal bloodline should make every Israelite want to keep the laws and statues. It's time to renew our mind in Yahawashi and prepare for His coming.

Romans 12:2 and be not conformed to this world: but be ye transformed by the renewing of your mind, that ye may prove what is that good, and acceptable, and perfect, will of Yahawah bahasham Yahawashi.

~ I ~

LEARNING THE TRUTH

Deuteronomy 4:1 Now therefore hearken, O Israel, unto the statues and unto the judgements, which I teach you, for to do them, that ye may live, and go in and possess the land which the LORD Yahawah God of your fathers giveth you.

If you are faithfully emerging yourself into your true heritage, friends and family will look at you like you are crazy and you may start to believe them. Here it is: a group of people come out of nowhere, saying they are waiting on a chariot to come from the sky and a large black man to save them. Sounds crazy right? You immediately think of some type of space invaders movie. You think of conspiracy theories, you think everything negative to associate it with Hebrew Israelites. But then you start to see prophecy unfold right before your eyes and see that you are not the crazy one after all.

You must keep yourself prayed up and occupied. Find a hobby that will actually make you happy whether you make money off it or not. It took me a long time to get used to actually being alone in this truth. I felt like nobody wanted to be around me anymore. I was always so upset because I already didn't have many friends, and all of my family are traditional church goers. Nobody wanted to talk to me about the Bible. However, the majority of people I know loved my old lifestyle and think that my new form of relaxation is quite boring. I always ask everyone why they feel the need to drink and participate in pagan activities, knowing that the spirits in both actually release demons. Demons that allow you to say and do things that you will never be able to get back. People just want to get the stress off of them, they don't believe they are real spirits, and they use their children as an excuse to celebrate the holidays. Now I must admit, when I was in the army, I drank every single day, unless I was deployed to Iraq or Afghanistan, then my drinks were down to about once a week. I would drink on my lunch hour, after work, on the weekends, you name it. All because I hated myself and I hated what I was doing with my life. I had such a hard time being around people. I grew up thinking if you drink, you'd have more fun. So that's what I did. I was living a very unhealthy lifestyle. All while still attending church faithfully.

After I stopped drinking and really started studying the word, I found it extremely hard to keep friends. I engulfed my life into the Bible. I would learn new scriptures daily and my husband would just look at me and smile. He always said it reminded him of when he first came into this truth. It's all I wanted to talk about and I always wanted to learn more. I had so many questions for him. All of my free time was devoted to this truth and my friends did not understand why. They didn't understand why I didn't want to go out or celebrate holidays anymore. Everyone started to believe that my husband changed me for the worse, when in all actuality, he just opened my eyes to the truth and changed me for the better. Arguments happened daily between my parents and I, and it actually hurt. Here I am trying to live by the laws of the Bible just to hear that what I'm learning is not the truth or done away with. I remember going to church a few years back to support my father and his sermon. I sat there so proud with my fringes and border of blue ready to dive into the scriptures my dad was about to give me. (Out of his 5 children, I was the only one that was able to make it.) However, the whole time he did nothing but tear down the Israelite name. Not only that, but they NEVER even cracked the Bible. His sermon lasted about 40 minutes on how the Israelites are a hate group that stands on the corner and chastises people. That was the last time I ever went to church.

How is it they always preach about coming as you are, but then do not accept the fact that we are the true Israelites? It is alright to have homosexuals, liars, and thieves in the church but not somebody who wants to learn the scriptures the right way? Why are we giving the church so much money, and we are not learning anything? Churchgoers around the world are depressed, living in poverty, or have ailing illnesses that prevent them from enjoying the outdoors and the pastors refuse to tell them why. They say we are no longer in biblical days but cannot tell us why we are still living with these devastations. Every word in the Bible has to be fulfilled and I don't know about anyone else, but I have not seen Yahawashi walking with us daily. I still see anger violence, wars, and prisons filling up with our people... So how is the law done away with if we are still being punished? How is the land of Israel righteous, if the people dwelling in that land do not believe in Yahawashi and serve false gods and idols? The true Israelites have been "free" since the late 1800s and marching since the 1900s and we are still the number one target for the modern day slave catchers aka the police officers. Marching down to Washington is not going to get us anywhere but to a stack of blue uniforms waiting to use their weapons against us. This country has never been united and it's sad to say it will never be. This country was built for destruction. Esau has used his blessing of the sword to capture, enslave and torture our people so that prophesy could be fulfilled. This country started off as a country every nation wanted to move to because of "the American dream", but now it is like that party school your parents begged you not to go to. A place everyone knows will end in destruction and an example to the nations of the world as too what not to do. It's the mother of all harlots, a laughing stock and embarrassment to all nations. **Revelation 17:5 And upon her forehead was a name written, MYSTERY, BABYLON THE GREAT, THE MOTHER OF HARLOTS AND ABOMINATIONS OF THE EARTH.**

I have learned more in the past seven years I've been with my husband, than the entire time I was going to church alone. It's mind boggling how much information is in this book if you read it through spiritual eyes. Everytime I learn something new, I try my best to apply it to my everyday life. **Hebrews 10:26 For if we sin willfully after that we have received the knowledge of the truth, there remaineth no more sacrifice for sins, 27 But a certain fearful looking for of judgement and fiery imagination, which shall devour the adversaries.** Here are a few changes I made to my life after reading the scriptures.

Dietary Habits: after reading **Leviticus 11**, (the entire chapter) I completely stopped eating anything that was unlawful. Which included pork, seafood and fish that did not have fins or scales. Luckily, I had a good start because my husband didn't have anything unlawful in his house. I would find myself reading the back of labels at the store making sure all my products were kosher and gelatin-free. Everything I wanted to buy became a google search at the store. I said goodbye to my all time favorite candy as I turned the package over and saw that indeed gelatin is in gummy bears. (My heart still aches from this) I mean come on, not only those, nerds too? Why?? Why do they have to push such delicious food that is abominable by The Most High? Someone close once told me that he was not going to hell for eating pork. Now, I understand there is no physical place called hell so he was somewhat telling the truth, however, there are deadly diseases that are linked to these abominable foods, and our people still don't understand why they are suffering.

Clothing habits: **Numbers 15:38 Speak unto the children of Israel, and bid them that they make them fringes in the borders of their garments throughout their generations, and they put upon the fringe of the borders a ribband of blue: 39 And it shall be unto you for a fringe, that ye may look upon it, amd remember all the commandments of the LORD Yahawah, amd do them; and that ye seek not after your own heart and your own eyes, after which ye use to go a whoring: 40 That ye may remember, and do all my commandments, and be holy unto your God.** After studying these verses, I manually cut fringes and used iron on hem tape as a border of blue on all my dresses. I looked into actually buying Israeliete dresses but they were all so expensive and if you're like me, that money could be used for bills, food, gas, or anything else we need to survive these days. **Deuteronomy 22:5 the woman shall not wear that which pertaineth unto a man, neither shall a man put on a woman's garment: for all that do so are abomination unto the LORD Yahawah thy God.** Understanding we are still in captivity, yes, I still do wear pants but only when I have too. I feel ALOT more comfortable wearing longer dresses. **1 Corinthians 11:5 But every woman that prayeth or prophesieth with her head uncovered dishonoreth her head: for that is even all one as if she were shaven.** I take praying to Yahawashi bahasham Yahawahsi very seriously. One thing I hate is seeing women pray with their heads uncovered. It may seem a little silly but if you can't follow a simple direction as to covering your head while praying, why should The Most High listen to you? **Proverbs 28:9 He that turneth away his ear from hearing the law, even his prayer shall be abomination.** If I am out with my husband and my head is uncovered, I will always ask him to pray for whatever it is I am thinking at that particular moment. (My head is usually covered when I'm out without him. Just my way of honoring the head of the house.)

Holidays: I stopped celebrating holidays as soon as my husband sat me down and showed me the pagan activities that were going on right in front of my face all these years. After doing research on birthdays, I soon saw that it's the highest of all satanic holidays due to the fact that you are highly reverencing yourself. **Ecclesiastes 7:1 A good name is better than precious ointment; and the day of death than the day of one's birth.** The day of your death, your spirit is sent back up to Yahawah and Yahawashi. This is one of the main reasons everyone always says they are in a better place. The day you are born, your spirit is sent back to the earth from our Heavenly Father to fulfill his will, not our own. (Also, Yahawashi didn't celebrate his birthday so why should we?) They told the world that Christmas is so called Jesus' birthday however when we read the Bible, he never celebrated nor do we know when he was actually born. Also, there's only one place in the bible that talks about having a tree in the center of your house and The Most High was warning us NOT to participate in it. **Jeremiah 10:3 For the customs of the people are vain:** vain meaning, unsatisfactory or emptiness. **For one cutteth a tree out of the forest, The work of the hands of the workman, with the axe.** A man cuts a tree with an axe, out of the forest that produces oxygen for us to breathe. **4 They deck it with silver and with gold: they fasten it with nails and with hammers, that it move not.** They beautify it with silver and gold and make sure it doesn't move. *5 They are upright as the palm tree, but speak not: they must needs be borne, because they cannot go.* You must take care of this tree. They will need to be picked up because they cannot walk on their own. *Be not afraid of them: for they cannot do evil, Neither , also is it in them to do good.* Do not be afraid of these trees, they cannot do any good or evil. The Most High said DON'T participate in this tradition and here we still have trees in every house, church, and business our people own.

They try to sell us on Thanksgiving by telling us they brought the tribe of Gad food instead of plaques, diseases and death. *Genesis 49:19 Gad, a troop shall overcome him: but he shall overcome at the last. Amos 5:21 I hate, I despise your feast days, and I will not smell in your solemn assemblies. 22 Though ye offer your meat offerings, I will not accept them: neither will I regard the peace offerings of your fat beasts.* The two most disrespectful pagan holidays and they still believe The Most High will be in the midst of them.

Halloween is the most demonic holiday out there but it pushes candy and fun on little children. They tell our children it's ok to dress up and be anything they want to be. *Exodus 22:18 Thou shalt not suffer a witch to live.* Also, *Leviticus 19:31 Regard not them that have familiar spirits, neither seek after wizards, to be defiled by them: I am the Lord Yahawah your God.* All these verses and extensive research showed me that the holidays we have been participating in our whole life, all derived from pagan rituals. Every single one of them. *Hosea 8:13 They sacrifice flesh for the sacrifices of mine offerings, and eat it; But the LORD Yahawah accepteth them not; Now will he remember their iniquity, and visit their sins: They shall return to Egypt.* I mean they even changed the times and began celebrating the new year in the dead of winter instead of the time of year that everything is new. They declared America's freedom July 4th, 1776, while the children of Israel were still in hard bondage. And the worst holiday of them all, while we are supposed to be celebrating the Passover, they instilled into us at a very young age to run around and look for eggs a giant bunny laid. We must research everything we have been taught and begin to live righteously. **1 Peter 1:22 Seeing ye have purified your souls in obeying the truth through the Spirit unto unfeigned love of the brethren, see that ye love one another with a pure heart fervently:** Main point verse **23 Being born again, not of corruptible seed, but incorruptible, by the word of Yahawah bahasham Yahawashi, which liveth and abideth forever.** Jumping down to verse **25 But the word of the Lord Yahawah bahasham Yahawahshi endureth forever. And this is the word which by the gospel is preached unto you.**

Now, does all this mean we have to stop watching our favorite shows or listening to our favorite music? Not at all! Once your eyes are opened, you will want to rewatch those shows that you love, just to see how they tie in with the Bible. (Television gets all their blockbuster ideas from the Bible and tribes of Israel.) As much as I study and constantly have lessons playing as I do things in and out the house, The Most High still wants you to take time for yourself. It even states in the bible that music and wine is good for you. **Sirach 40:20 Wine and music rejoice the heart: but the love of wisdom is above them both.** There is absolutely nothing wrong with continuing with habits you started before you came into the truth, as long as they are not a hindrance to your learning and do not steer you off path. I absolutely love cartoons, however I notice all the wickedness they are pushing to the kids. A few of my favorite movies and TV shows also twist the stories of the true Israelite Nation. For instance *"The Matrix series", "300", and "Once Upon a Time"* which is proof that they understand reincarnation.

So please, do not lose yourself as you gain your true identity. Waking up to the truth you start to see how The Most High have kept his angels encamped around you your whole life. You begin to see how many times you were upset by the outcome of something, just to find out that The Lord was protecting you from his wrath. All the evil that was thrown to you because you attended every single church service that came with a collection plate. Not just Sunday morning, we're talking about all the special services that make church last all day. Come out of the wicked ways of the world, and strive to live in Yahawashi's fold.

REVELATION 18:4 *And I heard another voice from heaven, saying, Come out of her, my people, that ye be not partakers of her sins, and that ye receive not of her plaques.*

After rewatching some of your favorite shows, do you notice how they take a lot from the bible?
Do you notice how they are pushing wickedness on children?

~ II ~

THE ISRAELITE MARRIAGE

1 Timothy 5:14 I will therefore that the younger women marry, bear children, guide the house, give none occasion to the adversary to speak reproachfully.

What exactly is marriage? Where do we get certain customs? And is a huge wedding worth the struggles that come after the ceremony? These are all the questions we as women must ask ourselves. Some women are so ecstatic to have a wedding, that they do not prepare to become a wife. My husband told me a few days after I moved in with him that it was us until the end, but then stated that he didn't want to get married in this kingdom. Of course at that time I was mad because I didn't understand what that meant. What was the point of us being together if it didn't end in marriage? However, our spirits were too connected for me to just let him go. There was just something about him that urged me to stay under his protection. Now, there was one verse in the bible that made me really want to go into a deeper study of being a wife. *I Corinthians 7:34 There is a difference also between a wife and a virgin. The unmarried woman* (an unmarried woman and virgin was the same thing when we kept the laws) *careth for the things of the Lord, that she may be holy both in body and spirit: but she that is married careth for the things of the world, how she may please her husband.* It really confused me because my husband was who I received my knowledge from. I wanted to be true to both my husband as well as the law. Well, I learned when a woman is married, she often takes after the customs and ways of her husband, and if he is not learning the true word of the Lord, then the woman would fall back into the world to please her man. This goes back to wanting a husband so bad you would do anything to keep him.

What did marriage mean to our heavenly father? Zondervan's Bible dictionary defines marriage as an intimate PERSONAL union to which a man and woman consent, consummated and continuously nourished by sexual intercourse, and perfected in a life-long partnership of mutual love and commitment. The Hebrew word **Onaw** means cohabitation; conjugal rights. (Living together; Drawn together through sexual intercourse) The Hebrew term **Laqah** means to take into marriage or to be drawn together as one. This is the reason the Bible speaks so much about the marriage between The Most High and the Israelites. *Revelation 19:7 Let us be glad and rejoice, and give honour to him: for the marriage of the Lamb is come, and his wife hath made herself ready.* It is speaking of being drawn together as one. Once the kingdom is established, we will be able to see the glory of The Most High Yahawah and his son Yahawashi will reign with us forever. But, we will go into that later. So, The Most High recognizes a man and woman drawn together as one who nourishes their union through intercourse, which often results in the procreation of children. *Genesis 1:27 So Yahawah created man in his own image, and in the image of Yahawah created he him; male and female created he them. 28 And God blessed them, and God* *said unto them, Be fruitful and multiply, and replenish the earth, and subdue it: and have dominion over the fish of the sea, and over the fowl of the air, and over every living thing that moveth upon the earth.* When you google the definition of marriage it says: 1. The legally or formally recognized union of two people as partners in a personal relationship (historically and in some jurisdictions specifically a union between a man and a woman). 2. A combination or mixture of two or more elements. Now how did we go from a personal union to a legally or formally recognized union? Why must we apply for a babylonian certificate in order to be with someone we love? When The Most High and The Powers made man and woman, he simply told them to be fruitful and multiply. That verse does not translate to, "Run down to the court real quick and get this paper notarized so I will know yall are truly one. No he said, roughly paraphrasing, have sex and produce children to rule over the earth. So again, why do we have to pay the government for a marriage license and throw an expensive wedding, just to obtain certification stating that our union is official? In ancient times, marriages were arranged mostly to act as alliances between households. The parents or authority figures would arrange the ceremony date, discuss the dowry and usually sign contracts to ensure the marriage was legit.

Here are some traditions the ancient Romans followed. Some are quite similar to the American kingdom we are living in today:

The Engagement Ring - Worn symbolically on the third left finger. The Romans believed that a nerve in that finger ran straight to the heart.

Age joined together - 12-14 years (As does with the Israelites) usually after the woman's first menstrual cycle.

Ceremony dates - The Romans believed in luck or omens not The Most High. They chose ceremony dates very carefully to avoid any ill omens. June was the primary month for weddings, while February and May were strictly forbidden.

Transfer of authority - Marriages transfers authority of the woman from her father to her husband. (As does with the Israelites) Once the woman gets married, she goes from learning the acts of being a wife from her mother or another female figure, to actually becoming a wife and putting what she learned to the test.

Consent - Consent of marriage was shown publicly afterwards to make the union official. Easiest way for the ancient Romans to do this was to hold hands in public.

Wedding - The wedding was typically at the fathers house consisting of no more than 10 people.

The Vows - The vows of the Romans were actually a chant. "Quando to Gaius, ego Gaia". (When and where you are Gaius, I then and the am Gaia.) They believed the name was lucky. Gaius: male name of latin origin meaning 'Person of the Earth'.

The offering - The bride and groom then made an offering to Jupiter, which usually consisted of cake.

The procession - A procession followed the new couple as nuts were thrown from behind. (Yes, nuts, not rice. Just imagine getting clocked in the head with nuts as you try to enjoy the first moments of being a wife.)

Over the threshold - Finally, the bride recites the consent chant once more, then is carried over the threshold. The bride lights a torch carried in front of the procession which is then blown out and tossed into the crowd who immediately scrambles for it. (I guess they were burnt one too many times and decided to go with soft flowers instead.)

Now sisters, who hasn't dreamt of a beautiful lavish wedding? A day where all the attention belongs to us? Sitting in a shop or room that smells like burning hair and high hopes for hours. Then pile on makeup until we look unrecognizable to everyone attending. Finally squeezing into a dress and heels that are definitely not comfortable, just to dance the night away as if the pain never existed. Well, now that we know where we get these pagan traditions from, let's see how our ancient ancestors celebrated a union.

Of course being the chosen nation of the Most High Yahawah, our laws are unconventional to many other nations. *Deuteronomy 14:2 For thou art a holy people unto the LORD Yahawah thy power, and the LORD Yahawah hath chosen thee to be a peculiar people unto himself, above that nations that are upon the earth.* It is stated again in *1Peter 2:9 But ye are a chosen generation, a royal priesthood, an holy nation, a peculiar people; that ye should shew forth the praises of him who hath called you out of darkness into his marvelous light:*

The woman had to be untouched - *Deuteronomy 22:13-21* explains what happens if a woman marries a man after having sexual relations before the ceremony. Main points. *Verse 20 But if this thing be true, and the tokens of virginity* (blood that is shed during first intercourse) *be not found for the damsel: Verse 21 Then they shall bring out the damsel to the door of her father's house, and the men of her city shall stone her with stones that she die: because she hath wrought folly in Israel, to play the whore in her father's house: so shalt thou put evil away from among you.*

Multiple wives - Israelite women could only have one husband, however, the man could have multiple wives. *Deuteronomy 22:22 If a man be found lying with a woman married to a husband, then they shall both of them die, both the man that lay with the woman, and the woman: so shalt thou put away evil* *from Israel.* If a woman were to cheat on her man, not only will she suffer the consequences but the other man as well. Multiple wives were typically chosen by the woman's father or one of the current wives would gift a wife to her husband. ***Genesis 16:3 and Sarai Abrams wife took Hagar her maid the Egyptian, after Abram had dwelt ten years in the land of Canaan, and gave her to husband Abram to be his wife.*** (I suggest you also read ***Genesis chapters 29 and 30*** to get a full understanding of how Jacob received all of his wives.)

Age of marriage - A woman was given into marriage after her first menstrual cycle, typically around 12-14 years of age. ***1Corinthians 7:36 But if any man think that he behaved himself uncomely toward his virgin,*** If a man is unsure if he should have sex with this young woman ***if she pass the flower of her age,*** if she has had her first menstrual cycle ***and need so require,*** and they want to have sex ***let him do what he will,*** let him have sex ***he sinneth not: let them marry.*** He is not doing anything wrong, let them join together as one through sexual intercorse.

The betrothal - The betrothal is what we call today, an engagement. A ceremony date would then be made and the two are not to have sexual intercourse until that day.

The ceremony - During the ceremony, which consisted of huge feats, the new groom and bride would then consummate their marriage (by having sex) and the groom would show the sheets proving she was a virgin. (blood stained sheets as stated in Deut 22:20). Yes, I know it sounds disgusting, but I'd rather show the token of my virginity than to be stoned by every man in the city.

Before we continue, let's break down exactly how Yahawashi's parents got married, and why it is such a hugely debated topic amongst people of all nations. Growing up we were taught that Mary was found with child before she laid with Joseph, which resulted in an immaculate conception. A virgin in the Bible is described as an unmarried woman. In those days there were no righteous women having sex before marriage. So once a woman had sex she was considered married. However, as it was stated earlier, the two are not to have sex until the ceremony date. So, before Yosep and Miriam made it to the marriage ceremony, they could not contain themselves and had sex. Remember, to marry is to be joined together as one. **Matthew 1:18 Now the birth of Yahawashi was on the wise:** (This is how the birth of Yahawashi went. On the wise simply means in this manner, thus or so) **when as his mother Miriam was espoused to Yosep** (Yahawashis parents were engaged and the marriage ceremony date was already set) **before they came together** (together as one union during the ceremony) **she was found withchild of the Holy Ghost** (they had sex and found out she was pregnant. Yosep is now Miriam's husband because they came together as one and Yahawashi's spirit was in Yoseps sperm.) Yosep was now afraid that she would be found not a virgin and stoned because there would be no proof of her token of virginity. **Matthew 1:19 Then Yosep her husband,** (Yosep is now Miriam's husband because they consummated and nourished themselves sexually,) **being a just man,** (Man who fears Yahawah greatly) **and not willing to make her a public example,** (Men of the village stoning her as in **Deut 22:21**) **was minded to put her away privily.** (He wanted to run away and hide her.) It wasn't until an angel appeared and basically told him, the seed that pushed through his loines is the savior of our nation. Matt 1:20-21 His spirit was then calmed and he knew him and his new wife and son were going to be safe. Matt 1:24-25. Yahawashi is also known as the seed of David, which means his fathers bloodline stems directly from King David. There is no way anybody could be connected to any nation on Earth without a man to implant the seed.

Inter Family Marriage - Marriage between cousins was typically normal between Israelites, however, immediate family was forbidden. (**Genesis 29** explains how Jacob was Leah and Rachel's cousin)

Fellow Israelites - Women could only marry one Israelite man of their families choosing. *Numbers 36:6 This is the thing which the Lord Yahawah doth command concerning the daughters of Zelophehad, saying, let them marry to whom they think best; only to the family of the tribe of their father shall they marry.* (Zelophehad had no sons but 5 daughters. They were to marry a man of the seed of Israel.) Israelite men were allowed to have the other nations as concubines. *1Kings 11:3 And he had seven hundred wives, princesses, and three hundred concubines: and his wives turned away his heart.*

Continuing Seed - If an Israelite husband died with no children, his brother was expected to marry the wife and bear his seed. *Deuteronomy 25:5 If brethren dwell together, and one of them die, and have no child, the wife of the dead shall not marry without unto a stranger: her husbands brother shall go in unto her, and take her to him to wife, and perform the duty of a husbands brother unto her. 6 And it shall be, that the firstborn which she beareth shall succeed in the name of his brother which is dead, that his name be not put out of Israel.*

Genesis 38:8 And Judah said unto Onan, Go in unto thy brothers wife, and marry her, and raise up seed to thy brother. 9 And Onan knew that the seed should not be his; and it came to pass, when he went in unto his brothers wife, that he spilled it on the ground, lest he should give his seed to his brother. 10. And the thing he did displeased the LORD Yahawah: wherefore he slew him also. That's also a message to us, stop telling your husband to pull out and trust that The Most High will protect your family. If you do not want to have your husband's child, why did you marry him?

And if you truly believe in The Most High Yahawah and his son Yahawashi, what are you afraid of?

Order of household - The husband will always be the head of the house, and we must respect that. *1 Corinthians 11: 3 But I would have you know, that the head of every man is Hamachiac; and the head of the woman is the man; and the head of Hamachiac Yahawashi is Yahawah. 1 Peter 3:1 Likewise ye wives, be in subjection to your own husbands; that, if any obey not the word, they also may without the word be won by the conversions of the wives. 1 Peter 3:5 for after this manner in the old time the holy woman also, who trusted in Yahawah, adorned themselves, being in subjection unto their own husbands: 6 Even as Sara obeyed Abraham, calling him lord: whose daughters ye are, as long as ye do well, and are not afraid with any amazement.*

Everything that has been written in our Holy Scriptures was written for this generation and the end is approaching quickly. Take heed to the scriptures and come back to the father. If you have a husband, let him lead. Yahawah bahasham Yahawashi wants his elect in the order he commanded in the bible, which means we as women must get back in our proper place.

Romans 15:4 For whatsoever things were written aforetime were written for our learning, that we through patience and comfort of the scriptures might have hope.

Do you understand the true meaning of marriage?

~ III ~

CUSTOMS OF THE WORLD

Mark 8:36 For what shall it profit a man, if he shall gain the whole world, and lose his own soul?

Now we see vast differences between traditional pagan customs and the customs of our ancient ancestors. We also understand what it actually means to marry and how these pagan customs crept into the lives of the Hebrew Israelites over the generations. I'm not saying that you cannot have that wedding that you have dreamed of, just remember **Ephesians 6:12 For we wrestle not against flesh and blood, but against principalities, against powers, against the rulers of the darkness of this world, against spiritual wickedness in high places.** The Israelites today are not fighting against individual people. We are fighting against the sins and evilness that this world wants us to participate in. A lot of these pagan rituals that we do participate in, we don't even understand we are referencing gods of other nations. **Exodus 23:33 They shall not dwell in thy land, lest they make thee sin against me: for if thou serve their gods, it will surely be a snare unto thee.** Things as little as celebrating holidays, going to concerts, even going to the gym all have pagan ancestry. ***Proverbs 4:19 The way of the wicked is darkness: they know not at what they stumble.*** Before celebrating anything, we must read up on where these customs derived and the true meaning of them. Things we do may seem harmless to us, but once we crack open this book, you will start to realize why The Most High is angry with the wicked. ***Job 9:24 The earth is given into the hands of the wicked: He covereth the faces of the judges thereof; If not, where, and who is he?*** The wicked have made everything against the Bible legal and pleasant to the eyes. Just as the treacherous one in the garden deceived Eve, that same spirit is back but now has the ability to deceive all nations. They have changed times, laws, identities, you name it! ***Daniel 7:25 And he shall speak great words against the Most High, and shall wear out the Saints of the Most High, and think to change times, and laws: and they shall be given into his hand, until a time and times, and the dividing of times.*** There were pagan rituals added to the calendar that coincide with our Holy days. Again, these pagan rituals seem fun and harmless so throughout the generations they have adapted to our lifestyle. Concerts, movies and live events all have secret messages the elite push out unto the world. Making the masses see what they want them to believe. They also have managed to strip us of our identity. ***Psalm 83:4 They have said, Come, and let us cut them off from being a nation; that the name of Israel may be no more in remembrance.*** Before The Most High sent us into slavery, we knew who we were and understood what was happening. It took generations for them to brainwash us and make us think we were of African origin with no power. They made us forget who our real savior is and what he looked like while walking the earth. Meanwhile they gave us blond hair blue eyes Jesus in return. ***1Maccabees 3:48 And laid open the book of the law, wherein the heathen has sought to paint the likeness of their*** *images.* Now every church you attend has the face of a different nation posing as our savior but will not preach on the following scriptures proving Yahawah, Yahawashi, as well as the chosen nation Israel were all dark skin.

Revelation 1:14 His head and his hairs were white like wool, as white as snow; and his eyes were a flame of fire; 15 And his feet like unto fine brass, as if they burned in a furnace; and his voice the sound of many waters.

Job 30:30 My skin is black upon me, and my bones are burned with heat

Lamentations 5:10 Our skin was black like an oven because of the terrible famine.

Song of Solomon 1:5 I am black, but comely, O ye daughters of Jerusalem, as the tents of Kedar, as the curtains of Solomon

Daniel 10:6 His body also was like the beryl, and his face the appearance of lightning, and his eyes as lamps of fire, and his arms and his feet like in the colour to polished brass, and the voice of his words like the voice of a multitude.

They have tried everything to take away our name, heritage and power. *Deuteronomy 28:37 And thou shalt become an astonishment, a proverb, and a by-word, among all nations whither the Lord Yahawah bahasham Yahawashi shall lead thee.* We have been called everything except the children of The Most High Yahawah. Niggers, coons, colored, spicks, wetbacks, redskins, indians, africans, and americans just to name a few. So if Jacob's seed is the righteous kingdom, and we know their skin color, what color is Esau/Edom's seed and his wicked kingdom? Just ask yourself these questions, who has the most military bases outside their country? Who invaded the most countries? Who profits most off the backs of other nations? There have been a lot of lies and cover ups, just so that we will continue on without our power. Centuries of passing laws and manipulating the minds of everyone, so they can push forth with their agenda. However, no matter how hard they try, this word will get through to The Most High's remnant. It has been prophesied, which means it MUST come to pass. **Baruch 2:27 O Lord Yahawah our power, hath dealt with us after all thy goodness, and according to all that great mercy of thine, 28 As thou spakest by thy servant Moses in the days when thou didst command him to write the law before the children of Israel, saying, 29 If ye will not hear my voice, surely this very great multitude shall be turned into a small number among the nations, where I will scatter them. 30 For I knew that they would not hear me, because it is a stiffnecked people: but in the land of their captivities they shall remember themselves.** The awakening of the Israelites started to move forward around the 1960s when our Elders began to wake up and really teach the nation of Israel. All 12 tribes. **31 And shall know that I am the Lord Yahawah their God** (power)**: for I will give them an heart, and ears to hear: 32 And they shall praise me in the land of their captivity, and think upon my name,** If you google Israelites around the world, you will see that there are a lot of camps in different countries calling out the name YAHAWAH bahasham YAHAWASHI. **33 And return from their stiff neck, and from their wicked deeds: for they shall remember the ways of their fathers, which sinned before the Lord Yahawah.** We are remembering what our forefathers went through for not keeping the laws. We understand the Bible is a history book, rule book, and prophetic book written by our forefathers for us today. **34 And I will bring them again into the land which I promised with an oath unto their fathers, Abraham, Isaac, And Jacob, and they shall be lords of it: And I will increase them, and they shall not be diminished.** Now that we are awakened to the fact we are indeed Israelites, Yahawashi will be returning sooner than people realize, to take us back to our land and make our men Kings and Priests over all the earth. *35 And I will make an everlasting covenant with them to be their God, and they shall be my people: and I will no more drive my people of Israel out of the land that I have given them.* The laws, statutes, and commandments will be the equivalent of blinking to the nation of Israel. We will be faithful to Yahawah bahasham Yahawashi and will forever reign in the land our father promised to us.

Before The Most High saves us from this captivity, we must start practicing the ways and true customs of the bible. Now, nobody is able to keep the law 100% because of the change of times and customs and due to the fact that we are surrounded by heathen nations. *Habakkuk 1:4 Therefore the law is slacked, and judgement doth never go forth: For the wicked doth compass about the righteous; Therefore the wrong judgement proceedeth.* However, we must start practicing the laws now, so The Most High knows we are ready to serve our true Power Yahawah and Lord Yahawashi. *Judges 5:11 They that are delivered from the noise of archers in the place of drawing water, There shall they rehearse the righteous acts of the Lord Yahawah, Even the righteous acts towards the inhabitants of his villages in Israel: Then shall the people of the Lord Yahawah go down to the gates.* That is the only way he will save us from the hell and bondage we are going through. We have to rehearse the righteous acts of the Lord Yahawah, wherever we may be scattered. We have to let go of what all religions have taught us and come back to our true power. *Proverbs 28:9 He that turneth away his ear from hearing the law, even his prayer shall be abomination.* This is one verse the traditional church will never share with its members. The real reason we are still struggling with poverty, hunger and a desire for the american dream is because we are not keeping the biblical law. If you stop calling on Jesus, Yeshua, Yashia etc. and ask Yahawashi, I guarantee you one million percent if you truly believe in this Bible, (the Bible that was written for so-called Blacks, Hispanics, and Native Americans) you will get everything you ask for and more. But you must take the bitter as well as the sweet. Gulp it down and pray to Yahawah that he gives you the strength to endure the test and trails you are about to go through.

Isaiah 47:4 As for our redeemer, The LORD Yahawah of hosts is his name, the Holy One of Israel.

What pagan rituals will you give up after learning the true word?

~ IV ~

FROM WOMEN COME WICKEDNESS

(The Mother of all Nations)

Sirach 42:12 Behold not every bodies beauty, and sit not in the midst of women. 13 for from the garments cometh a moth, and women wickedness

Why are we considered the weaker vessel in the Bible? *1Peter 3:7 Likewise, ye husbands, dwell with them according to knowledge, giving honour unto the wife, as unto the weaker vessel, and as being heirs together of the grace of life; that your prayers be not hindered.* First, I must say, there are a lot of harsh words used towards the women of Israel in today's kingdom, especially the sisters of Judah. That is because we have been conditioned into thinking that the world revolves around us. Throughout the years, Esau has given the Israelite women so much in exchange for the absence of the Israelite man. *Jeremiah 31:22 How long wilt thou go about, O backsliding daughter? For the LORD Yahawah hath created a new thing in earth, A woman shall compass a man.* We have been given a feminism movement which in turn gave women an 'I don't need a man for anything' mindset. Every time we celebrate the first Israelite female to accomplish something, we are one step higher on Esau's ladder. The same ladder he has placed over the Israelite man for centuries. Now, wanting to be humble and obedient to your husband is looked upon as a bad or strange thing. Like, the husbands have wives locked in the basement waiting for a bell to ring to fulfill his every desire. They changed the entire format of a family and then decided to legalize it. But hey, The Most High Yahawah made it that way for His purpose. We don't understand everything that The Most High does and it is not for us to understand. It states in *Judith 8:14 For ye cannot find the depth of the heart of man, neither can ye perceive the things that he thinketh: then how can ye search out Yahawah, that hath made all these things, and know his mind, or comprehend his purpose? Nay, my brethren, provoke not the Lord Yahawah our power to anger.* For a long time, I wondered why Yahawah made me a servant. Why did I have to be the weaker vessel. But as you can see, everyone is back in their lot and has their specific purpose in The Most High's movie we call life.

Now, I had to look up this word weaker in the Blue Letter Bible. The Blue Letter Bible is an app and website you can go to, that will break down the definition of the word in the language it was written in. The word weaker is defined as weak, infirm, or feeble. Infirm is defined as: not physically or mentally strong, especially through age or illness. So from the very beginning, The Most High stated that we are not as physically or mentally as strong as the Israelite man. He made everything the way he wanted for a reason. *Ezekiel 34:30 Thus shall they know that I am the LORD Yahawah their God am with them, and that they, even the house of Israel, are my people, saith the LORD Yahawah power.* Main point *verse 31 And ye my flock, the flock of my pasture, ARE MEN, and I am your Power, saith the LORD Yahawah*

power. Yahawah's flock and Yahawashi's treasure are the true men of Israel. The men who know who they are and try to follow the scriptures to the best of their abilities. The man's treasure is the woman. We are a gift from the Lord Yahawah Bahasham Yahawashi to the man. Which is why one of our punishments is that our husband shall rule over us. Now let's dive into why we are considered the weaker vessel, why we received this punishment in the first place, and how it ties in with the modern day Israelite woman scattered among the nations in the earth.

The Mother of All Nations

When I was younger, I never understood the story of Adam and Eve and how it would be so significant during the last days. It honestly helped me understand how Eve represents the Israelite woman and why we are compelled to do certain things. Every nation wants to study the origin of Adam and Eve but nobody wants to read the bible through scriptural eyes. Nobody but the traditional church believes that Eve sat there and spoke with an actual snake. This is because the church will not teach you that there were other people walking the earth with Adam and Eve. Adam and Eve were the first two people to have the spirit of the Yahawah dwelling in them. When you look up the word serpent, it goes back to the Hebrew term Nachach: which just means serpent or snake. Now when you google the actual definition of serpent, the second definition that comes up is <u>A sly or treacherous person, especially one who exploits a position of trust in order to betray it.</u> Now that we understand that Eve was not speaking with an actual snake, but to a sly and treacherous person, we can move on. ***Genesis 2:17 But of the tree of the knowledge of good and evil, though shalt not eat of it: for in the day that thou eatest thereof thou shalt surely die.*** The tree of good and evil actually represented different philosophies and doctrines outside the garden where the Most High placed them.

Adam and Eve were still in their immortal bodies in the paradise Yahawah made just for them. **2 Corinthians 11:3 But I fear, lest by any means, as the serpent beguiled Eve through his subtilty, so your minds should be corrupted from the simplicity that is in Hamachiach.** That same spirit that lied to Eve, is back today lying to the entire world. (We also know that both Adam and Eve came from outside the garden because he placed them back where they came from when they were kicked out. **Genesis 3:23 Therefore the LORD Yahawah power sent him forth from the garden of Eden, to till the ground from whence he was taken.**) Also, Ecclesiastes 10:11 compares a serpent to a babbler so we know that he was a smooth talker. **Eccl 10:11 Surely the serpent will bite without enchantment; and a babbler is no better.** The top sales people in the world are usually smooth talking men. So we can understand why Eve was so tempted. Women have always loved to talk. I can imagine Adam being in the garden enjoying all The Most High gave to him, meanwhile here comes this sly, treacherous person babbling about all these doctrines and philosophies of the outside world. Eve was just like the typical Isaraelite woman today. She saw something that looked good, smelled, good, and had ways to give both her and her husband infinite knowledge, and it was FREE!?! (So she thought) When we as women come across something so nice, pleasant to the eyes, and it's cheap, we are quick to load it up, no matter how awkward or heavy that particular item is. **Genesis 3:6 And when the woman saw, that the tree was good for food, and that it was pleasant to the eyes, and a tree to be desired to make one wise, she took of the fruit thereof, and did eat, and gave also unto her husband with her, and he did eat.** The issue was, she should have consulted with her husband first. I do believe if she would have just gone to Adam and said "Babe, this dude told me to eat this apple that came off the tree The Most High forbade. Can you go talk to him real quick?" Adam would have gone straight up to him, "Hey bruh, you are NOT supposed to be here! Trespassing in the garden The Most High made just for me!" He would have then kicked him out, passed The Most Highs test, and we would all still be in our glorious bodies, living luxurious lives. But of course that's not the way it went. Because Eve decided to listen to the serpent, The Most High placed three curses on all women. <u>Three curses that prove our main duty as a woman is to become a wife.</u>

1. Excruciating pain with childbirth
2. The desire (longing/craving) shall be over the husband.
3. The Husband shall rule over us.

Genesis 3:16 Unto the woman he said, I will greatly multiply thy sorrow and thy conception; in sorrow thou shalt bring forth children; and thy desire shall be over they husband, and he shall rule over thee. Now, we as women hate the fact that our man has to rule over us and be the head of the household. But if you continue reading verses 17-19 The Most High was more angry at Adam for something Eve did. This whole spiral and downfall of man, Including our Israelite Kings, Princes, and Lords, as well as everything that happened to Yahawashi, was all because Eve did not consult with her husband. The serpent knew not to go to Adam because men are not as gullible as women are. But he knew Adam would listen to his wife. If you really think about it, we only received one major punishment. Childbirth pain. The other two wouldn't be as bad if both parties in the relationship tried to the best of their ability to keep the laws, statutes and commandments of the Holy Scriptures. The only thing The Most High did not strip them of was their living soul and their beautiful melanated skin tone.

So women have been the weaker vessel since Eve, however it was designed by Yahawah for His purpose. So no matter how we feel about being the weaker vessel, docile servants and help meets under the subjection of our husbands... We have got to get over it! The Most High is not going to change his mind no matter how many marches we participate in, how many men are "me tooed" or how many cultures are canceled.

Ecclesiastes 7:26 And I find more bitter than death the woman, whose heart is snares and nets, and her hands as bands: whoso pleaseath Yahawah shall escape her; but the sinner shall be taken by her.

Are you really ready to be submissive to a man of Yahawah Bahasham Yahawashi's choosing?

~ V ~

CONDUCTING YOURSELF AS AN ISRAELITE WOMAN

Sirach 7:19 Forgoe not a wise and good woman: for her grace is above gold.

Every woman who enters and continues in this walk, loves to find out that, not only are we a part of the Chosen seed of Yahawah and Yahawashi, but we are biblically, the most beautiful women in the entire world. *Jeremiah 6:2 I have likened the daughter of Zion to a comely and delicate woman. Judith 10:19 And they wondered at her beauty, and admired the children of Israel because of her, and everyone said to his neighbor, Who would despise this people, that have among them such women? Surely it is not good that one man be left who being let go might deceive the whole earth.* Majority women tend to slide when they see how much they will have to give up. I must admit, it was extremely hard when I began my walk. Everything has been thrown my way to steer me off course and test my faith. The biggest stumbling block I always ran into were the closed ears of those around me. It hurt me alot as I grew in my journey to hear what I am learning is false, hate doctrine, or I just sound crazy. It took a lot of prayer and scriptures from my husband to show me that I was going to lose a lot of friends and family on my Hebrew journey. ***Job 19:19 All my inward friends abhorred me: and they whom I loved are turned against me. Luke 21:16 And ye shall be betrayed both by parents, and brethren, and kinsfolks, and friends; and some of you shall they cause to be put to death.*** It became easier over time as I started to realize that our people really do not have access to this knowledge like many of us and they will not want to accept it. ***Hosea 4:6 My people are destroyed for lack of knowledge, Because thou hast rejected knowledge, I will also reject thee, thou shalt be no priest to me: Seeing thou hast forgotten the law of thy God Yahawah, I will also forget thy children.*** If you do not keep the laws and commandments given by The Most high, why should he protect you? Let's say for example, your name is Maria and you have come up with a cure for cancer. You tell people exactly what to avoid and how to live a long and healthy life. If they continue to call you Jessica, while going against everything you said, you will start to ignore them and eventually you will cut them off. That is the same what our Father and Yahawashi feel when we go to church and pray to Jesus or whatever false idol they may worship.

So how do we get back in the good graces of The Most High? Well, the first and most important step is to understand our role as a woman is not the same as a man. We must understand the Fathers order before we can get anything right. ***1 Timothy 2:11 Let the woman learn in silence with all subjection.*** Women be quiet and obedient. ***12 But I suffer not a woman to teach nor usurp authority over the man, but to be in silence.*** Women are not to be teachers or any type of government figure over the Israelite man, but to be in silence. ***13. For Adam was first formed*** *then Eve.* The Most High's possession is Adam. He only gave Adam a woman because he did not want him to be alone. So he created a weaker vessel for him. *14 And Adam was not deceived, but the woman being deceived was in the transgression.* Women are easily manipulated, therefore our man must have authority over us. The Most High gave us specific directions on what to teach and the rest is up to the men of Israel. They are the ones waking up the scattered Israelites. They are the ones on the highways and byways spreading the word of truth and The name of The Most High Yahawah. I'm pretty sure everyone has noticed by now, Yahawashi's disciples were all men. Yes, women were in the fold and followed Yahawashi as well, **Matthew 27:55 *And many women were there beholding afar off, which followed Yahawashi from Galilee, ministering unto him:*** However, the 12 chosen people that Yahawashi taught the truth, secrets, and prophecies to were men. We have a specific, more delicate role in the fathers eyes, but don't get it twisted! Yahawah and Yahawashi love us as well! Our job as women is to teach the younger women how to actually be wives to our men while they are out there doing the work of the Lord Yahawah. The Most High wants a peaceful union so that his chosen will be able to dwell in peace. ***1 Corinthians 7:3 Let the husband render unto the wife due benevolence: and likewise also the wife unto the husband.*** The word benevolence means good will, kindness, euphemistically (by means of a mild or indirect word or expression instead of one considered too harsh or blunt) and conjugal duty. So, we are to be kind to each other at all times, no arguing, no cursing and uniting our souls through intercourse occasionally. It is stated again ***Colossians 3:19 Husbands, love your wives, and be not bitter against them.*** The Most High did not put us together so we can argue everyday about the little things in the union.

There have been plenty of times I would get upset when my husband told me I couldn't do something. I didn't understand that he was actually trying his best to protect me. If I did it anyway, it seemed like the punishment from The Most High was always instant. Once actually sent me to the hospital and He even punished others around me if they were involved! (Now if that doesn't make you believe I don't know what will.)

1 Peter 4:17 *For the time is come that judgement must begin at the house of Yahawah: and if it first begin at us, what shall the end be of them that obey not the gospel of Yahawah?*

There are laws for anything you could think of in our Bible, a lot of which you can incorporate into your daily life. For instance, I know you have noticed once you came into the truth, you begin praying more than you ever have. But did you know there are certain ways that we are to pray?

Praying

Proverbs 28:9 He that turneth away his ear from hearing the law, even his prayer shall be abomination. If you are not trying your best to keep the laws of The Most High Yahawah, he will not listen to your prayers, nor will He bless you.

2 Chronicles 6:38 If they return to thee with all their heart and with all their soul in the land of their captivity, whither they have carried them captives, and pray towards their land, which thou gavest unto their fathers, and toward the city thou hast chosen, and toward the house which I have built for thy name: We are still in captivity. First thing to always remember while praying, we pray towards our homeland Israel, which means when we pray we should be praying towards the east.

1 Corinthians 11:5 But every woman that prayeth or prophesieth with her head uncovered dishonoureth her head: for that is even all one as if she were shaven.

1 Corinthians 11:13 Judge in yourselves: it is comely that a woman pray unto Yahawah uncovered? A woman praying with her head uncovered is the most disrespectful thing you could do. I cringe when I see a woman praying uncovered.

Matthew 6:6 But thou, when thou prayest, enter into thy closet, and when thou hast shut the door, pray to the Father which is in secret; and they Father which seeth in secret shall reward thee openly. Some people love getting attention while praying and they believe they need to be seen/heard from all people. No need to scream or shout in the middle of a huge prayer circle to be seen. The Father would rather you pray in secret, with no one around.

Matthew 6:7 But when ye pray, use not vain repetitions, as the heathens do: for they think that they shall be heard for their much speaking. 8 Be not therefore like unto them: for your Father knoweth what things ye have need of, before ye ask him. Vain repetitions means to stammer. To repeat the same thing over and over and over again. Babbling, trying to take up as much time as they can. The Most High doesn't need all of that. He knows what you need before you even think to ask. Verse 9 goes into The Lord's Prayer, which I will share with you in our Hebrew Tongue. The Holy Language (read right to left)

.Yahawah shamka hayah qadash shabashamayam Ahbanawah

.bashamyam hayah kawa baahrataza ishah hayah ratazahka thabaah Malakwathka

.kalyawam lachaam Nathanlanawa

.chaawabwathyanawa kasalachnawa chawabwathnawa Waslach-lanawa

.ri mayan hawashinawa ahbal banasayawan thabayaahnawa Walaah

Ahman ,laiwalamyam wahathapaahrath wahaahla hamalawath laka Kaya

Sex, Menstraul Cycles, and Childbirth

These are just a few laws explaining how we dealt with washing after sex, menstral cycles, and childbirth.

Leviticus 15:18 The woman also with whom man shall lie with seed of copulation, they shall both bathe themselves in water, and be unclean until even. I know its common sense, but when you have sex, you must bathe ourselves afterwards.

Leviticus 15:19 And if a woman have an issue, and her issue in her flesh be blood, she shall be put apart seven days: and whosoever toucheth her shall be unclean until the even. When I said we cant keep the laws 100% this is one of the verses I am speaking of. If you come on your period technically you are to leave your husband's house for 7 days. The next few verses go on to say that everything we touch, sit, or lie on is unclean until it is washed.

Leviticus 15:28 But if she be cleansed of her issue, then she shall number to herself seven days, and after that she shall be clean. No matter if you are one of those women whose cycle lasts only three perfect days, you are still unclean until the full seven days are up.

Leviticus 20:18 And if a man shall lie with a woman having her sickness, and shall uncover her nakedness; he hath discovered her fountain, and she hath uncovered the fountain of her blood: and both of them shall be cut off from among their people. Do not have sex during your period. It's disgusting.

Leviticus 12:2 Speak unto the children of Israel, saying, If a woman have conceived seed, and born a man child: then she shall

be unclean seven days; according to the days of the separation for her infirmity shall she be unclean. 3 And in the eighth day the flesh of his foreskin shall be circumcised. 4 and she shall the continue in the blood of her purifying three and thirty days; she shall not touch no hallowed thing, nor come into the sanctuary, until the days of her purification be fulfilled. If you give birth to a boy, you are unclean for 7 days, and on the eighth day you are to have him circumcised. Once he is circumcised, you are then unclean (as if you were on your cycle) for an additional 33 days. *5 But if she bear a maid child, then she shall be unclean two weeks, as in her separation: and she shall continue in the blood of her purifying threescore and six days.* If you give birth to a girl, you are unclean for 2 weeks, and then are unclean for an additional 66 days.

As I stated before, we are still in captivity so it is hard to keep the laws in today's society. These are just a few examples to prove that we once had order in our nation and actually kept these laws.

Now if you do have a man living the laws to the best of his ability, being an obedient woman is not hard. Does it get annoying? Absolutely! Who wants to serve, cook, and clean all day? That's not something little girls yelled out when we were asked what we wanted to be when we grew up. However, as I am elbow deep in dishwater, or banging pots and pans, scriptures are constantly running through my mind. *Sirach 26:3 A good wife is a good portion, which shall be given in the portion of them that fear the Lord Yahawah.* Or my favorite scripture, which is one of the reasons I treat my husband like a King. *Sirach 26:26 A woman that honoureth her husband, shall be judged wise of all: but she that dishonoureth him in her pride, shall be counted ungodly of all.* If I just try my best to keep these laws, hopefully

The Most High will have mercy on my soul and save me from his coming wrath. *1 Timothy 2:15 Notwithstanding she shall be saved in child-bearing, if they continue in faith and charity, and holiness, with sobriety.* This one verse is why I try my best to fulfill my duties as a wife. When I was younger, I always wanted seven children. My grandma has 10 and my mom has 5. I picked a number in the middle, not knowing that 7 just meant completion throughout the Bible. In 2017 I suffered an ectopic pregnancy. The pain I endured during that time was the worst, both mentally and physically. My husband was working in California while I suffered without him in Michigan. Not to mention my best friend had her baby 2 months prior, and my dog had her puppies the day after I arrived home from the hospital. I shut the world completely off because the one thing I wanted in life, I can't even produce. Through everything, I continued to keep my faith in Yahawah bahasham Yahawashi, and understood that each person's hell is just different afflictions. Mine is the inability to have children. *Jonah 2:2 And said, I cried by reason of mine affliction unto the LORD Yahawah, and he heard me; out of the belly of hell cried I, and thou hardest my voice.*

One of the main duties as a wife is to be the keeper of the house. Another lie we have been taught is that a marriage is 50/50 when in all actuality it is 100/0. *Ephesians 5:22 Wives, submit yourselves unto your husbands, as unto the Lord Yahawah. 23 For the husband is the head of the wife, even as Hamachiac Yahawashi is the head of the church: and is the savior of the body. 24 Therefore the church is subject unto Hamachiac Yahawashi, so let the wives be to their own husbands in everything.* Basically, the same way Yahawashi is the head of the church of Israel and will protect the children of Israel, that's the same way the men of Israel are over their wives and will do anything to protect them. The men of The Most High are not on the streets every week trying to be equal or higher than Yahawashi. No, they are reverencing him, praising him, and doing work for him. That is how it should be for us. We should be reverencing our man, praising him and doing the work that is needed around the house as we are commanded.

Still want to run things, argue, and belittle our men? **Proverbs 21:9** and **Proverbs 25:24 It is better to dwell in a corner of the housetop, than with a brawling woman in a wide house.** So, we actually see this verse twice in the same book. A man could be living in a huge mansion, but would rather go chill in the little creepy attic than to be around a woman that is arguing.

Proverbs 21:19 It is better to dwell in the wilderness, than with a contentious and an angry woman. We already know between Jacob and Esau, Jacob was the one who liked to chill in the house. Esau is the one who likes all that outdoorsy stuff. **(Genesis 25:27)** We also know that a lot of our men go fishing just to get some peace and quiet.

The household is not the only place where we practice being a chosen woman of The Most High Power. We have to remember during our day to day who we are representing. Yes, we are representing The Father and The Son, but first, we are a representation of our husbands. We are the glory of our husbands and we should be proud of that. When we walk out the house, we should not be contemplating on how many looks we may get or what man may try to stop and talk to us. We should be dressed in modest apparel. **1 Timothy 2:9 In like manner also, that women adorn themselves in modest apparel,** To properly reverence our man, we must adorn ourselves in clothing that doesn't have other men breaking their neck to get a peak. Now, I get it sometimes it's hard to cover up what the Most High blessed us with. We as Hebrew women have been blessed with the curves our men love, but when you try your best to cover up and only let your man see what belongs to him, Yahawah will see the effort you are putting in to be a better Israelite woman. Small things like that make a huge difference in The Most Highs eyes. The best feeling I get is being out in public and me and a fellow sister lock eyes because we noticed the fringes and borders of blue at the hem of our skirt. You think you are alone but there are sisters out there trying to do the same work as you. **With shamefacedness and sobriety;** When we are out with our man, we want the world to know that he is our protector. You are not loud, argumentative and most importantly not drunk. The word shamefacedness breaks down to modesty, bashfulness, reverence, respect, regard for others. We are not fighters. The saying "act like a lady" originated from the laws and statues the Israelite woman kept when we were in our glory. WE are supposed to be an example for these other nations on how to act like a woman. *not with broided hair, or gold, or pearls, or costly array;* When you understand the truth, you are not worried about getting your hair done every month, or buying the latest jewelry and clothing. Yes The Most High may bless you with those things but they are not something you are thinking of 24/7 **10. But (which becometh women professing godliness) with good works.** When you leave the house, you should always have the laws of The Most Highs in your heart, reverencing Him throughout the day. If you are trying your hardest to keep these laws, I guarantee, when Yahawah sends Yahawashi in those chariots, He will fight for you.

Sirach 4:28 Strive for the truth unto death, and the Lord Yahawah bahasham Yahwashi shall fight for thee.

Will you practice The Lord's Prayer in Hebrew daily?

~ VI ~

LONGING TO BE A WIFE

Psalms 107:9 For he satisfieth the longing soul, and filleth the hungry soul, and filleth the hungry soul with goodness.

Now there is a huge difference between wanting a husband and actually wanting to be a wife. Early on in life, I wanted a husband so bad that I did not seek The Most High first. I just wanted to get married and finally have a baby. A baby that I have been wanting since I was 17 years old. I never thought about the duties I would fulfill as a wife, I just thought about carrying life and fulfilling my duty as a mother. I even looked into in vitro fertilization when the army told me I wouldn't be able to get pregnant. Soon after I married a man I met in the army, I found out he was very abusive both physically and mentally. Growing up I thought it was normal for a man to be abusive. I fugured that's what it meant by a man being dominant over his woman. Sadly, it was embedded into what I thought was a normal relationship. I thought every wife went through the touture I saw as a child. I soon jumped right back into another abusive relationship. A relationship that could have led to my death. I remember I prayed to God that he just remove this man from my presence so I could move on with my life. I was so tired of the pain, scars and hurt left by many years of abuse. Within a month, the mother of his child personally drove 500 miles to pick him up and take him home. What a blessing that was for me! Now remember, during these times, I was still calling on Jesus and going to church every sunday. It wasn't until I was blessed with a man who wanted me to know the true name of our Lord and savior that I saw how a man is supposed to treat his wife biblically.

There is a saying that goes, '*Men marry women hoping they dont change, women marry men hoping they do.*' When in all actuality, the man is the one who stays the same, (habits, way of living, etc.) and it's normally the woman who changes. These changes could be positive toward the relationship or it could be a hindrance if we do not fully understand the roles and duties as a wife. If a woman was to keep the law biblically, the way our Father instructed us, there should be no issues within the household. Now when I say biblically I don't mean the traditional way of reading the Bible, you know those women who only use one or two verses and tell the entire congregation that they are the perfect wife. **Ephesians 5:25 Husbands, love your wives, even as Hamachiac Yahawashi also loved the church, and gave himself for it;** Women take this verse and think they can force their man to basically give them what they want. They do not break the scripture down and really understand what it means. **1 Timothy 3:5 (For if a man know not how to rule his own house, how shall he take care of the church of God?)** So the man has to know how to rule his house, his kingdom, his domain in order to be able to take care of the men of Israel that may fall beneath him. A man cannot lead, a strong boisterous, Yahawah fearing army, and in the middle of his speech, here comes his babbling wife, upset that he didn't wash the dishes. ARE YOU SERIOUS? **Psalms 101:6**

Mine eyes shall be upon the faithful of the land, that they may dwell with me: he that walketh in a perfect way, he shall serve me. So the church that Hamachiac Yahawashi loved in **Ephesians 5:25**, are the faithful of the land. The ones that are following the laws, statutes and commandments to the best of their ability. Which means, both parties should be following in the ways of The Most High in order for the husband to be able to love his wife/wives as Yahawashi loves the church.

Another verse that women love to use is **Proverbs 31:10 *Who can find a virtuous woman? Her price is far above rubies.*** Ruth was the only woman in the Bible who was called virtuous. Miriam wasn't even called virtuous and she is the actual birth mother of our Lord and savior. So why was Ruth so virtuous? Because she kept every single commandment of The Most High. Not only that, but when Naomi told Ruth to return to her mothers house, (Moab, today known as the so-called Chinese people), she told her that she was going to stay by her side no matter what. ***Ruth 1:16 And Ruth said, Intreat me not to leave thee, or to return from following after thee: for wither thou goest, I will go; and where thou lodgest, I will lodge: thy people shall be my people, and thy God my God.*** So Ruth saw the power of the only living God, The Most High Yahawah and would not leave her mother in law Naomi's side because of it. ***Sirach 26:3 A good wife is a good portion, which shall be given in the portion of them that fear the Lord Yahawah.*** No matter what nationality women are, if they prove that they will follow all the laws of The Most High, he will bless you with a true man of the Lord. ***Ruth 4:10 Moreover Ruth the Moabitess, the wife of Mahlon, have I purchased to be my wife, to raise up the name of the dead upon his inheritance, that the name of the dead be not cut off from among his brethren, and from the gate of his place: ye are witnesses this day.*** Ruth was not mad that she was purchased. How was she purchased?

Ruth 4:7 Now this was the manner in former time in Israel concerning redeeming and concerning changing, for to confirm all things; a man plucked off his shoe, and gave it to his neighbor: and this was a testimony in Israel. 8 Therefore the kinsmen said unto Boaz, Buy it for thee. So he drew off his shoe. 9 And Boaz said unto the elders, and unto all the people, Ye are witnesses this day, that I have bought all the was Eimelech's, and all that was Chillon's and Mahlon's, of the hand of Naomi. Ruth was bought by her husband with a shoe. All the land her former husband had was handed over for a shoe. Ruth was not upset at all. She praised The Most High for a man who follows the laws, statutes, and commandements. So yes, let's try to be like Ruth. Humble, obedient, and in our proper place.

The Israelite man has so much to deal with on a daily basis. Every other nation that looks at our men see them as unacceptable, thugs, poor, grimy, you name it. They think they could get over on our men and dumb them down to their standards of the world. They have to deal with bosses, both male and female, who look down on them because of their position in a company. Even when he gets a moment to relax in his vehicle, he has to be aware of his surroundings. Always on the lookout for police or other nationalities who may view him as a threat and take his life. He is in that situation everytime he leaves the house. Most men hate talking when they get home so you may never even know what's going on. Which is why The Most High gave him a help meet, so that when he comes into the house at the end of his day, he has the rest that is needed. A clean, pleasant smelling house. A meal prepared upon his welcome, and a wife who is not complaining about worldly things. Now, we must always understand this, only men who know they are indeed the true Israelites, will be able to lead us properly. It is so hard for women to keep the laws biblically if our covering is not grounded firmly in Yahawashi. The energy that is formed in the relationship is the energy that will be released out. If you have a man that is constantly studying the word and trying to live righteously, the foundation of your relationship will be rooted in Yahawashi. I guarantee it.

Another thing that we must understand, we are a possession from The Most High to the men of Israel. It sounds harsh, but WE DO belong to our husband. ***Ecclesiasticus/Sirach 36:24 He that getteth a wife, beginneth a possession, a help like unto himself, and a pillar of rest.*** There's a running joke I have with my best friend, when my husband wakes, I am clocked in for the day. I love my husband and I will do anything that does not disobey the laws of The Most High for him. I don't mind being a part of his property. Now if the woman decides that the true word of the Lord is not important, and tries to run the house herself, the foundation will not be stable and eventually the structure will fall and crush everyone in your household. ***Proverbs 14:1 Every wise woman buildeth her house; but the foolish plucketh it downe with her hands.***

Another highly debated topic we must get into, is a man having multiple women. I know, I know, nobody wants to share their men with anybody. But guess what? That's not what it says in the Bible. A great way of being a virtuous woman, is accepting the fact that your husband is free to have another woman. Notice that I did not say allow. We are not the ones that allow our husbands to do anything. We must accept the facts of the scriptures as they are written. We see plenty of times our forefathers had multiple wives. Prime example is Jacob's wives. Leah and Rachel were sisters, Bilhah and Zipah were their handmades. Leah gave birth to Reuban, Simeon, Levi, Judah, Issachar, Zebulon and Jacobs only daughter Dinah. Bilhah gave birth to Dan and Naptali. Zilpah gave birth to Gad and Asher. Rachel, who was the love of Jacob's life, birthed Joseph. ***Genesis 30:26 Give me my wives and my children, for whom I have served thee, and let me go: for thou knowest my service which I have done thee.*** Once I understood that multiple wives is indeed biblical, I prayed for that spirit of jealousy away. ***Isaiah 4:1 And in that day seven women shall take hold of one man, saying, we will eat our own bread, and wear our own apparel: only let us be called by thy name, to take away our reproach.*** In that day is referring to the day Yahawashi comes back, which means, during Jacob's trouble, there will be multiple women with one Israelite man. So begin praying that spirit of jealousy away. Stop reading the bible with your emotions and start reading through scriptural eyes. There is no such thing as one woman for every man, each Israelite man is given a complete amount for his desires. They are Kings and Priests of The Most High and deserve whatever He chooses to give them. And as for copulation habits, PLEASE YOUR MAN! Begin treating him like the King he is. As long as he is not asking you to invite a third person or begs you for backdoor play, the bedroom is undefiled. ***Hebrews 13:4 Marriage is honourable in all, and the bed undefiled: but whoremongers and adulterers Yahawah will judge.*** The sacred union between a man and woman is honorable and the bedroom is not defiled. Meaning what you do with your husband is not dirty and you do not lose purity because of it. However, the male prostitutes, and those who are unfaithful to Yahawah, Yahawashi as well as their husbands, are the ones who will receive the wrath of The Most High Yahawah.

Proverbs 31:30 favour is deceitful, and beauty is vain: but a woman that feareth the LORD Yahawah, she shall be praised.

Are you ready to be virtuous?

~ VII ~

ISRAELITE WOMAN SUMMARIZED

Exodus 1: 19 And the midwives said unto Pharaoh, Because the Hebrew women are not as the Egyptian women; for they are lively, and are delivered ere the midwives come in unto them.

There are vast differences between Hebrew women and women of every other nation. We have specific rules, laws and customs to follow for a reason. Every law that was given to us, was given to keep us safe and disease free, that's how much Yahawah and Yahawashi loves the nation of Israel. All the rules of being an Isrealite woman can be summed up in **Titus 2:3-5**. This is a scripture I did hear in the church growing up, however when you break it down and understand it, you begin to notice how the older women of the church still gossip, drink, lie, run the streets, and are all up in other men's faces.

Titus 2:3-5
3. The aged woman likewise, that they be in behavior as becometh holiness, not false accuser, not given to much wine, teachers of

good things; 4. That they may teach the young women to be sober, to love their husbands, to love their children, 5. To be discreet, chaste, keepers at home, good, obedient to their own husbands, that the word of Yahawah be not blasphemed.
So let's break it down: **Verse 3. The aged woman likewise,** Older women, this is how we are to behave. **That they be in behavior as becometh holiness.** Becometh holiness is broken down to the Greek word hieroprepes (hee-er-op-rep-ace) meaning befitting men, places, actions or sacred things to Yahawah. So basically, we are to be appropriate in all ways including to our man. **Not False accuser,** in the Greek word diabolos, meaning, prone to slander, slanderous accusing falsely. Aka Liars for no reason. **Not given too much wine.** It's ok to drink a little wine from time to time, even a small glass of that strong drink if you need it. But as chosen women of The Most High Power Yahawah, we are to conduct ourselves as such. NOBODY likes a stumbling drunk, loud, "black, hispanic or native american" female. Especially our God! **Teachers of good things.** Teaching young women (not men!) how to conduct themselves and how to be a holy wife to their husband in these last days.
Verse 4 That they may teach the young women: (again not men!) Now is the time for the Israelite sisters to get ourselves together. We know for a fact that there will be more women saved than men, and we know that by the complete number of wives each chosen man will have entering into the kingdom (***Isaiah 4:1 And in that day seven women shall take hold of one man, saying, We will eat our own bread, and wear our own apparel: only let us be called by thy name, to take away our reproach.***) Which means IT WILL start on this side. So we must get used to this now. No matter how much we may hate sharing our man, it is biblical. (It took me YEARS to be ok with this, and some days, I still find myself praying that spirit of jealousy away.) **To be sober.** Again,

The Most High and our Israelite Kings and Priests hate stumbling drunk women. *To love their husbands.* (The way the Most High commanded us too) I have 3 pitbulls, and every time my husband wakes up or pulls into the driveway, we are all excited. That's how it should be, you shouldn't hear him coming down and you are already cussing him out in your head, you should be happy he is awake, ready to assist him. *To love their children.* Not with just your words (*1John 3:18 My little children, let us not love in word, neither in tongue; but in deed and in truth.*) Be an example to your children, especially our little girls. My best friend always says she is the first example for her daughters and they take mental notes of everything she does. From how she makes her money, to the way she lives her life, even the men that she dates. And that is so true. If you are setting a positive example for your babies and they see how the Father is rewarding you, they will do anything to be just like their mother.

Verse 5 To be discreet, Greek word sophron: so-fron meaning: of a sound mind, sane, in one's senses, curbing one's desires and impulses, self-controlled, temperate. Growing up I thought discreet meant secrecy, the lies we have been told. We must have a mind following the laws and curb the desire to do evil. If you ever have to persuade yourself that what you are doing is not a sin, more than likely it is. Now sisters, this is going to be tremendously hard. Everytime you learn something new, you have to apply it to your everyday life, but we know we are still in captivity and in some cases, that will not be possible. *Habakkuk 1:4 Therefore the law is slacked, and judgment doth never go forth: For the wicked doth compass about the righteous; Therefore the wrong judgment proceedeth.* **Chaste,** Greek word hagnos: hagnos meaning 1. exciting reverence, venerable, sacred. 2. Pure - pure from carnality. (wordly) modest. Pure from every fault, immaculate, clean. Come out of the world. No matter how hard it may be. Trust that Yahawah bahasham Yahawashi will provide your every need. **Keepers at home,** caring for the house, working at home. The watch or keeper of the house. Keeping at home and taking care of household affairs. My husband always explained to me how we are still in captivity so it is extremely hard to keep the laws 100%. So up until the middle of 2021, I have worked constantly. I noticed as I was working, that's when me and my husband would argue the most. I would start the arguments but at the time I didn't understand that I really was not fulfilling my duties as a wife. I was always upset because I was so tired, I didn't feel like cooking or cleaning. I finally prayed and asked The Most High to allow me to be a better wife. I was so tired of working. Especially during a pandemic. I felt like I was the only person in the world still getting up at 4 am to prepare for work. It wasn't until The Most High sent an angel to allow me to completely retire at the age of 35. Since I have been home everyday, we have had no arguments. I love having the house clean and ready for use before he wakes up. I love cooking for him and making sure his area is always clean. I actually love my new job. As soon as my husband wakes up I clock in for the day. Whatever he needs, I'm there. **Good, obedient to their own husbands.** The word obedient comes from the Greek word hypotasso: hoop-ot-as-so. 1. To arrange under, to subordinate 2. To subject, put in subjection. 3. To subjects oneself, obey. 4. To submit to one's control. 5. To yield to one's admonition or advice. 6. To obey, be subject. Now, just because I "clock in" when he wakes up, doesn't mean I have much to do. He does not ask alot at all. I'm usually doing my own thing until he asks me to hand him something or when he gets hungry. Females always think I'm chained up, only to be let out when he needs something. Before the pandemic started, I absolutely hated going out. I loved being in the house learning about something that actually has relevance to our lives. When I prayed to be a better Israelite woman, The Most High gave me a chance to be obedient, to be subjective and to obey my husband. He even gave me the spirit to allow my husband to have another wife, as long as it is done biblically and he is able to take care of both households. *That the word of Yahawah be not blasphemed.* Blasphemed Greek word blasphemo: blas-fay-meh-o meaning 1. to speak reproachfully, rail at, revile, calumniate. 2. To be evil spoken of.

So now, Titus 2:3-5 has been broken down line for line. There should not be any issues on what it means to be an Israelite woman in these last days. It should be something we are striving for. If you pray to our Heavenly Father, he will allow you to be an Israelite woman the correct way. You will learn that being submissive and subjective to your husband is not a bad thing as long as you are following the laws of The Most High God. Of course, there are times that you could be doing everything in your power right, and The Most High will still send his left hand side to test your faith. You must hold your faith through everything that you go through. The Book of Susanna in the Apocrypha is an excellent example.

Now Susanna was a very beautiful young woman married to a very wealthy man named Joicim. She learned the laws and statues from her parents and kept them to the best of her ability. She was one of those righteous women, who was given to a very righteous man. Now at the same time, we still have wickedness going on in the world as we do today. There were two wicked elder judges that were appointed that year and they were very amazed at her beauty. *Susanna 1:8 And the two elders saw her going in every day and walking; so that their lust was inflamed towards her.* These men were breaking the law because they were lusting after a woman they knew was married. *(Matthew 5:8 But I say unto you, That whosoever looketh on a woman to lust after her hath committed adultery with her already in his heart.)* So here is this beautiful woman, minding her own business in her husband's garden, meanwhile we have two creeps hiding in the bushes stalking her every move. **Susanna 1:14 So when they were gone out, they parted the one from the other, and turning back again they came to the same place; and after that they had asked one another the cause, they acknowledged their lust: then appointed they a time together, when they might find her alone.** They didn't want to tell each other at first, but they ended up in the same spot trying to get a glance. They came up with a plan that was a win-win in their head. **Susanna 1:19 Now when the maids were gone forth, the two elders rose up, and ran unto her saying, 20 Behold, the garden doors are shut, that no man can see us, and we are in love with thee; therefore consent unto us, and lie with us. 21 If thou wilt not, we will bear witness against thee, that a young man was with thee: and therefore thou didst send away thy maids from thee.** The elders made a plan to force her into having a threesome with them when everybody left. So Susanna had a choice. She could either sleep with both these men and fulfill their weird, twisted fantasy, or not sleep with them and they tell the town she had an affair with another man. They thought they had her cornered. **Susanna 1:22 Then Susanna sighed, and said, I am straitened on every side: for if I do this thing, it is death unto me: and if I do it not I cannot escape your hands.** They knew for a fact she would just concede and let them have their way. Who knows, they may have done this with other women in their previous terms. Instead, she keeps her faith in Yahawah knowing that he will save her from these men. **Susanna 1:23 It is better for me to fall into your hands, and not do it, than to sin in the sight of the Lord Yahawah. 24 With that Susanna cried with a loud voice: and the two elders cried against her.** Everyone believed the elders story, even her husband was upset and wanted her put to death. This was one of those bad times in Israel's history when the man's word meant more than the womans. We are a weaker vessel so of course we would lie right? Susanna kept her faith even when they condemned her to death. **Susanna 1:41 Then the assembly believed them as those that were elders and judges of the people: so they condemned her to death. 42 Then Susanna cried out with a loud voice and said, O everlasting power, that knowest the secrets, and knowest all things before they be: 43 Thou knowest that they have borne false witness against me, and behold, I must die; whereas I never did such things as these men have maliciously invented against me.** The rest of the chapter describes how Daniel saved her just by asking these men, "What tree was she under?" That simple question saved Susanna's life. She had no idea how, but she knew The Most High would send an angel down to save her. She never lost her faith or cursed Yahawah because of what she was going through. Can you imagine having your hands tied, escorted down the street by huge muscular men, just so they could have the entire male population of the village stone you because they believe you are a harlot. (By the way, those wicked elders were put to death according to the law.)

Just like The Most High tested Job, he did the same with Susanna. Now Susanna should be a female in the Bible that we all look up too. The faith that she has is the faith that we should feel every single day. I love my husband with all of my heart, but just loving him is not going to get me to the kingdom. At the end of the day, you have to take a long, hard look at yourself. If Hamachiac came today, would he call me his Ahchwath? (Sister) Or would he scare the living soul out of me by saying, I never knew you? This is why our Hebrew journey has to be constant. This is why we have to learn not just the sweet parts of the Bible, but the bitter parts as well. True Hebrew Israelite elders, apostles, and teachers understand that the woman does not run anything and they are not afraid to show it. This is why women tend to listen to false Israelite groups that will lead them astray. However, the true Israelite Elders also reassure the FEW sisters that are taking notes and learning. One of the apostles always says "If it doesn't apply to you, you won't get offended." And guess what? I don't. I never get offended and to the women out there trying their best to do the right thing, you shouldn't either. It is a beautiful thing when a new soul has come back to the fold, but you have to take the good with the bad, beautiful and ugly, blessings and curses. You have to eat of the entire scroll and endure to the end to be saved. He already said these times would be the toughest times that Israel has ever seen. ***Daniel 12:1 And at that time shall Micheal stand up, and the great prince which standeth for the children of thy people: and there shall be a time of trouble, such as never was since there was a nation even to that same time: and at that time thy people shall be delivered, every one that shall be found written in the book.*** We have got to stay rooted in Yahawashi and (if you are married) follow our husbands orders. We can see all prophecies being fulfilled. From the various plaques swarming the earth, to the Euphrates river drying up. The door is closing to this spiritual ark and just like in the days of Noah, the devastation is coming quicker than people think. So remember ladies, ***Sirach 9:12 Delight not in the thing that the ungodly have pleasure in; but remember they shall not go unpunished unto their grave.*** Come out of the worldly traditions of man and back to following the laws, statutes, and commandments of The Most High God Yahawah. We know that this world is at its end because of the signs that are around us. Yahawashi explained to us exactly when he is coming back so we better be prepared. You don't want to be caught living unrighteously just because you think you have 10 or 20 years left. This kingdom is not our rest. *Micah 2:10 Arise ye, and depart; for this is not your rest: because it is polluted, it shall destroy you, even with a sore destruction.* This kingdom is the punishment The Most High warned us about in the book of **Deuteronomy 28:68.** *And the LORD Yahawah shall bring thee into Egypt again with ships, by the way whereof I spake unto thee, Thou shalt see it no more again: and there ye shall be sold unto your enemies for bondmen and bondwomen, and no man shall buy you.* The Most High Yahawah warned us that if we did not keep the laws and commandments that He gave us, he would send us into slavery again by ships, longing for our homeland. He allowed our enemies to overtake us and put us into slavery making sure no man would buy us. (Hebrew word qanah meaning redeem or save). Yahawashi is the only one that can save us from this hell we are forced to live in and he is coming back very quickly, and he's coming back for vengeance. Which side do you want to be on?

Joshua 24:15 And if it seem evil unto you to serve the LORD Yahawah, choose you this day whom ye will serve; whether the gods which your fathers served that were on the other side of the flood, or the gods of Amorites, in whose land ye dwell: but as for me and my house, we will serve the LORD Yahawah.

When was your faith tested the most?

~ VIII ~

YAHAWASHI'S COMING QUICKLY

Luke 17:26 And as it was in the days of Noe, so shall it be also in the days of the Son of man. 27 They did eat, they drank, they married wives, they were given in marriage, until the day Noe entered the ark, and the flood came, and destroyed them all.

Signs can be seen worldwide of the coming of our savior. The disciples specifically asked Yahawashi how would we know that Esau's kingdom was coming to an end, and when we will be back in our rightful glory? *2Esdras 6:9 For Esau is the end of the world, and Jacob is the beginning that followeth.*

Matthew 24:4-14

1. *And Yahawashi answered and said unto them, Take heed that no man deceive you.* (Do not believe these liars.)
2. *For many shall come in my name, saying, I am Hamachiac; and shall deceive many.* (There will be a lot of brothers

coming out that saying I am anointed and will make many believe their lies)

3. *And ye shall hear of wars and rumors of wars: see that ye are not troubled: for all these things must come to pass, but the end is not yet.* (You will hear of WW1, WW2 and the buildup of WW3 all the wars in between. But do not be afraid. All of these wars must happen but the end is not yet.)

4. *For nation will rise against nation, and kingdom against kingdom: and there shall be famines, pestilences, and earthquakes in diverse places.* (The people will fight against their government, the EU will fight amongst each other: people will starve, viruses and plaques will come about, and earthquakes in places many didn't expect.)

5. *All these are the beginning of sorrows.* (This is the beginning of Jacob's trouble.)

6. *Then shall they deliver you up to be afflicted, and shall kill you: and ye shall be hated of all nations for my name's sake.* (Israelites; so called blacks, hispanics, and native americans will be held in bondage, beaten, tortured, imprisoned, and killed. All because you are an Israelite of Yahawah bahasham Yahawashi.)

7. *And then shall many be offended, and shall betray one another, and shall hate one another.* (Israelites will be enticed to sin and friends and family will start to hate you.)

8. *And many false prophets shall arise and deceive many.* (There will be people you think are prophets of the Most High Yahawah but will still lead the people of Israel astray.)

9. *And because iniquity shall abound, the love of many shall wax cold.* (Because the true law of the Lord is not being

established, love that once ruled the land will be turned into hatred and war.)
10. **But he that shall endure to the end, the same shall be saved.** (But the Israelites who have faith and follow the commandments to the best of their ability, these are the ones who will be called up into the chariot.)
11. **And this gospel of the kingdom shall be preached in all the world for a witness unto all nations; and then the end shall come.** (The gospel of the Kingdom of Yahawah bahasham Yahawashi will be taught by the true prophets of Israel in every country Israelite resides, to testify to every nation that stems from Abraham, and then the end will come.)

Yahawshi told us exactly what will happen right before he comes in his glory to pick us up. Everything he has said has happened except the mark of the condemned and the final war, which we know is right around the corner. ***Revelation 13:16 and he causeth all, both small and great rich and poor, free and bond, to receive a mark in their right hand, or in their foreheads: 17 And that no man might buy or sell, save he that had the marke, or the name of the beast, or the number of his name.*** Ladies, we have got to get it together. So called blacks, hispanics and native american women, it's time. Esau's Kingdom is not going to last forever and it has already started crumbling. Come out of the ways of the world and back to our power. The power who is coming to save his chosen and to punish the wicked. ***Luke 17:28 Likewise also as it was in the days of Lot; they did eat, they drank, they bought, they sold, they planted, they builded; 29 But the same day that Lot went out of Sodom it rained fire and brimstone from heaven, and destroyed them all.*** When people think about the world ending, they think of the entire world exploding, alien invasions, or some catastrophe that wipes out civilization. The

Bible states that other nations will see the downfall of America, which means, only one country will be completely destroyed and inhabitable. *Revelation 18:8 Therefore shall her plaques come in one day; death, and mourning, and famine, and she shall be utterly burnt with fire, for strong is the Lord Yahawah, who judgeth her. 9 And the Kings of the earth, who have committed fornication, and lived deliciously with her, shall bewail her and lament for her, when they shall see the smoke or her burning: 10 Standing afar off for the fear of her torment, saying, Alas, alas, that great city Babylon,* (America) *that mighty city: for in one hour is thy judgement come.*

Revelation 18:21 and a mighty Angel took up a stone like a great milestone, and cast it unto the sea, saying, Thus with violence shall that great city Babylon be thrown down, and shall be found no more at all.

I pray that I was able to reach The few Israelite sisters that needed this. Stayed prayed up and continue to watch the times. The Lord Yahawashi is coming back very soon. 2020 marked the year of the Caragma, 2021 marked the year of Hasting, and 2022 has been marked the year of Yahawashi turning up, so we have got to be prepared. We have already seen signs in the heavens as well as on earth. Let's get off our high horse, trade in those wicked queen of heaven crowns for the royal princess crown Yahawashi will present to his elect on that flight out of here. Qam Yasharahla!! (Arise Israel) Our redemption draweth near!!

2 Esdras 2:27 Be not weary: for when the day of trouble and heaviness cometh, others shall weep and be sorrowful, but thou shalt be merry and have abundance.

Are you ready for Yahawashi's return?

~ IX ~

ROMANS 13:11

Romans 13:11

Our world is in chaos fulfilling all prophecies they teach. Kidnap, murder, enslavement, but still won't let us speak.
America's brutal past, our forefathers had to bear it. Fast forward to the future, our torture you will inherit.
We have not forgotten our laws, we remember our holy ways. We refuse to spend money on your vanity Pagan days!
Turning off the TV and opening the Great Book, you began to read and understand how the biblical Jews look.
They have hair like mine, dark skin as well. Explains our slavery here and how and why we fell.
Shows us how to eat and how to live right, It even explains when we should or should not fight.
This book gives us hope for the morning, and blessings throughout the day, although this world is collapsing, we have our faith to know the way.
This book is full of secrets, only a few can decipher. If only they knew it was orchestrated by Higher.

To open The Eyes Of The Remnant seed, to prove to non-believers our inheritance is guaranteed.
But Hebrews refuse to accept the knowledge of our salvation. They claim to read the Bible, but won't break down Revelation.
Celebrating the pagan days, as if it's a tradition for our nation, not abiding by the holy days, that's truly our occasion.
Praising the sodomites, as if they're not our enemy. After realizing the truth, how can they be a friend to me?
My mind has been opened, I see dreams and visions. Making my walk my number one mission.
Cracking the book and revealing its secrets, trying to find out why the world did not teach us.
Where we came from and where we belong, Who we were before, and where we went wrong?
My LORD has hair like wool and burnt brass colored feet, the images we've been taught, now who could this be?
We have been fooled by the media, which is controlled by the elite. Once Israel rises the prophecy will be complete.
The punishment for sin is just too huge to hide. So just like that Edom decides to lie.
Enslave us to the system, but let us believe we are free. If we had just kept the laws, think where we'd be.
We'd live without feminists, we'd live without the Klan, wed never have to work for the devilish white man.
We have been stolen from our land and enslaved to their laws, beaten and tortured to cover up their flaws.
The first time we saw him we were fleeing from Egypt. This time around he's gathering from all regions.
Not an eye will miss him, all heathens will wail at the site of The Most High knowing he will prevail.

When that Lion roars and you see fangs and claws... Just know Yahawah bahasham Yahawashi will destroy Esau.
He's coming for blood and also for vengeance, Romans 13:11 Israel it is time to pray for repentance.
We're almost to our glory, alongside our LORD. Praising him daily, never getting bored.
No tears to wipe away, not one eye to dry, no reason for sadness, All Praises to The Most High!!!

Romans 13:11 And that, knowing the time, that now it is high time to awake out of sleep: for now is our salvation nearer than when we believed.

~ X ~

12 TRIBES CHART

12 Tribes Chart

So called Negroes, Hispanics, and Native Americans have been scattered throughout every country in the world. This chart does not mean there are no Israelites in Africa, China, Japan etc... This is just where majority of Israel live to this day

Name/Tribe	Hebrew pronunciation	Meaning
Ruban=Seminole Indians	Ra-aw-ban	See its a son
Simeon=Dominicans	Sha-mi-wan	Affliction Heard
Levi=Haitian	Law-ya	Joined to me
Judah=Negroes	Ya-ha-wa-dah	Yahawah Thanks
Benjamin - West Indies	Ban-yah-man	Son of the right hand

Naptali=Argentina to Chileans	Na-pa-thal-yah	My wrestlings
Gad=Native Indians	Gad	Troop
Asher=Brazil to Columbians and Urauguayans	Ah-shar	Happy
Issachar= Mexicans	Yash-sha-car	He is hired
Zebulun=Panama to Guatemala	Za-ba-la-wan	Dwelling
(Joseph)Ephraim=Puerto Rico	Ah-pa-ra-yam	I am fruitful
(Joseph)Manasseh=Cuba	Ma-na-shah	Causing to forget

Shalawam Yasharahla!

www.ingramcontent.com/pod-product-compliance
Lightning Source LLC
Chambersburg PA
CBHW071838290426
44109CB00017B/1858